THE REAL-LIFE
FINANCIAL RESOURCE
GUIDE FOR YOUTH

TEEN & YOUNG ADULT EDITION

CONTENTS

FOREWORD

When I founded Ella's Angels, my vision was simple: to create opportunities for young people and give them the tools to succeed. One of the most important tools — and one of the least taught — is financial literacy. I've seen firsthand how many of my peers don't learn about money until they're already facing debt, credit cards, or student loans. By then, mistakes are expensive. I wanted to create a resource that speaks to us — teens and young adults — in a way that's real, simple, and practical. This book is not financial advice. I'm not a financial advisor, CPA, or lawyer. This is an educational guide — something to help you understand the basics of money so you can make better choices. Whether it's figuring out your first paycheck, applying for a credit card, or saving for your future, my hope is that these chapters give you clarity and confidence. At Ella's Angels, we believe in education, empowerment, and building pathways for the next generation. Financial literacy is part of that mission — because money should be a tool you control, not something that controls you. Read this book with an open mind. Ask questions. Talk with your family and trusted professionals. But most importantly: take action. Even small habits — like saving a few dollars from every paycheck — can change your future. This book is dedicated to every young person ready to take control of their future. May it inspire you to build not just wealth, but independence, confidence, and peace of mind.

— Ella Shahbazian
Founder, Ella's Angels (501c3)

01

WHERE DID MY PAYCHECK GO?

You finally got that paycheck... and it's way smaller than you expected. Who's taking your money? Short answer: the government. But before you panic, here's the breakdown — and why it's actually good news if you learn to play the money game early.

Federal Income Taxes

Everyone pays, but how much depends on your income bracket. For 2025 (single filers): 10%: $0 – $12,750

12%: $12,751 – $53,500

22%: $53,501 – $102,000

24%: $102,001 – $183,000

32%: $183,001 – $235,000

35%: $235,001 – $578,125

37%: $578,126+

"Progressive" means you only pay the higher rate on the portion of income that falls into that bracket — not your entire paycheck.

Social Security & Medicare (FICA Taxes)

6.2% ➔ Social Security: Money you pay now helps today's retirees. When you retire, you'll collect monthly benefits too (earliest at 62, full benefits around 67).

1.45% ➔ Medicare: Funds healthcare for seniors. Together = 7.65% of every paycheck.

Think of Social Security as a safety net, not your entire retirement plan.

State Income Taxes

Not every state taxes income. In fact, 9 states don't: Alaska, Florida, Nevada, South Dakota, Texas, Washington, Wyoming, Tennessee, and New Hampshire.

The others range anywhere from 1% (North Dakota) up to 13.3% (California).

Visuals

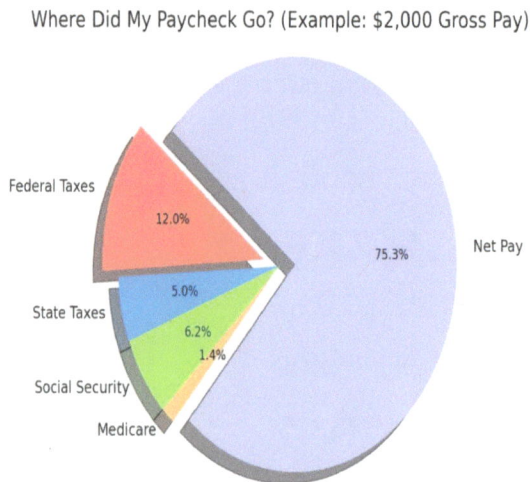

Where Did My Paycheck Go? (Example: $2,000 Gross Pay)

Money Gifts & Saving Smart

You can receive up to $18,000 per year (2025) as a money gift from someone — totally tax-free.

If you get cash gifts (birthday, graduation, etc.), save at least part of it. Let compound interest do the heavy lifting:

- Save $1,000/year from age 15 to 35 and let it sit.
- By age 65, it could grow to over $450,000.

But if you save consistently — even just $100/month from age 15 all the way to 65 — your account could grow to about $545,000.

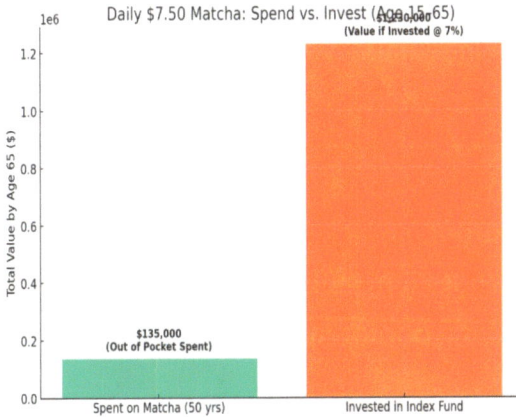

Daily $7.50 Matcha: Spend vs. Invest (Age 15–65)
(Value if Invested @ 7%)

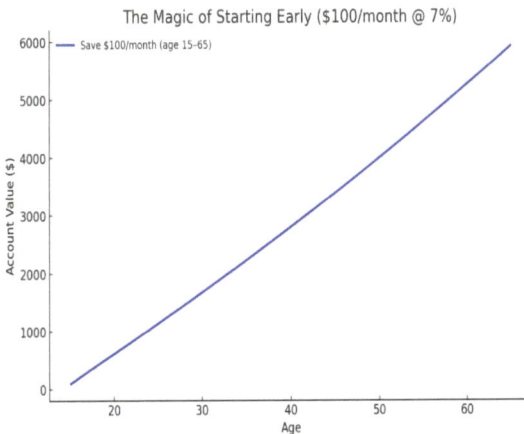

The Magic of Starting Early ($100/month @ 7%)

Millionaire Math: Your Favorite Large Matcha

A daily $7.50 "favorite large matcha" = about $225/month.

If you invested that instead in an index fund averaging 7% return from age 15 to 65:

- You'd have about $1.23 million.
- Plus, you save yourself the cavities and the calories.

Example Paycheck Breakdown

Always check your paystub:

- Gross pay = what you earned.
- Net pay = what actually hits your bank account.

Mini Checklist

- ☐ Look up your state's tax rate
- ☐ Find your federal bracket
- ☐ Add 7.65% (FICA) to estimate real take-home pay
- ☐ Save at least a portion of every gift or paycheck

Takeaway Quote

"Your gross pay is a fantasy. Your net pay is reality."

Business Basics: Where Does Your Money Live?

Now that you know how much actually lands in your hands, let's talk about where that money goes next.

Savings Accounts

A place to stash money you don't want to spend right away. Pays you a little interest. Best for emergencies or goals.

Checking Accounts

Your everyday spending hub. Comes with a debit card. Fast access to money but usually no interest.

Debit Cards

Connect directly to your checking account. Swipe = money leaves instantly. Safer than cash.

Bank Fees

Watch for overdraft, ATM, and minimum balance fees.

Credit Unions

Member-owned, often lower fees and better interest. More community-focused.

Mini Checklist (Add-On)

☐ Open both a checking and a savings account

☐ Use your debit card responsibly (it's not free money)

☐ Avoid unnecessary bank fees

☐ Compare your bank vs. local credit unions for the best deal

Takeaway Quote

"Getting a paycheck is exciting, but keeping it and growing it is the real power move."

02

CREDIT SCORES & CREDIT BUREAUS

Your credit score is like your adult GPA — but instead of teachers grading you, it's banks, landlords, and even some employers. Behind the scenes, three big credit bureaus are keeping score. A good score can save you thousands of dollars. A bad score? It'll cost you.

What a Credit Score Is

- A 3-digit number (ranges from 300–850). Higher = better.
- Tells lenders how risky it is to let you borrow.

What Affects Your Credit Score

- **Payment History (35%)** → Pay on time, always.
- **Credit Utilization (30%)** → Keep under 30%.
- **Credit Age (15%)** → The longer your accounts are open, the better.
- **Mix (10%)** → Variety of cards/loans helps.

- **New Inquiries (10%)** ➜ Too many applications hurt.

Who Tracks Your Score (Credit Bureaus)

The "Big Three" credit bureaus are like referees of the financial world:

- Equifax
- Experian
- TransUnion

They:

- Collect info from banks, credit card companies, lenders, and landlords.
- Create your **credit report** (history, balances, new accounts).
- Provide data to lenders when you apply.

Why Credit Bureaus & Scores Matter

- Your score is based on their reports.
- Mistakes happen ➜ a wrong late payment or fraud can hurt you.
- You're legally entitled to a free report each year from each bureau (AnnualCreditReport.com).

Smart Credit Habits

- Pay bills on time (set auto-pay).
- Keep balances low.
- Don't apply for too many cards.
- Check reports annually and dispute errors.

QUICK TIP

Missing just one payment can tank your score for years — always pay at least the minimum.

Mini Checklist

☐ Pay bills on time.

☐ Keep balances <30% of your limit.

☐ Review credit reports annually.

☐ Dispute errors quickly.

☐ Know the three bureaus: Equifax, Experian, TransUnion.

Takeaway Quote

"Your credit score is your financial reputation — and the credit bureaus are the reporters. Protect it like your iPhone."

Visuals

Credit Score Factors

- New Inquiries — 10%
- Credit Mix — 10%
- Credit Age — 15%
- Payment History — 35%
- Utilization — 30%

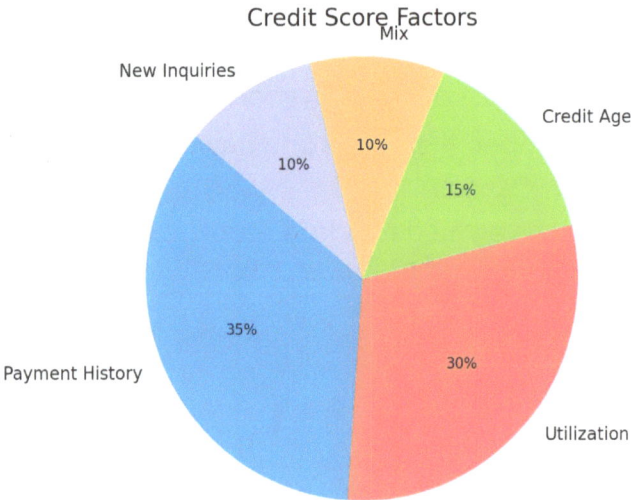

The Big Three Credit Bureaus

Equifax

Experian   TransUnion

How Credit Data Flows

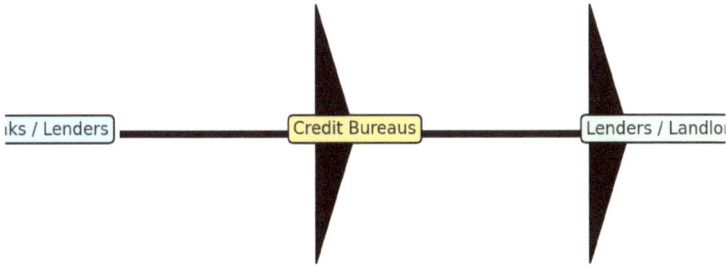

```
ıks / Lenders ————————  Credit Bureaus  ————————  Lenders / Landloı
```

Annual Credit Report Reminder

> Reminder:
> Check all 3 credit reports
> once per year
> (AnnualCreditReport.com)

Credit Score Reminder

> Quick Tip:
> One late payment can
> hurt for years!

03

CREDIT CARDS & DEBT

Getting your first credit card can feel like freedom — but it's also a test. Used wisely, a credit card builds your financial reputation. Used carelessly, it can trap you in debt fast. Credit cards are like fire — super useful if controlled, but dangerous if left unchecked.

What to Know Before Applying

- You must be 18+ (or 21+ without income).
- Under 21? You'll need a co-signer or proof of income.
- Approval depends on your credit history — tricky if you're just starting out.

Best First Card Options

- **Student Credit Card** ➜ For young adults with little/no history.
- **Secured Credit Card** ➜ Deposit = your limit.
- **Authorized User** ➜ Join a parent's card to build credit.

What Lenders Look At

- Credit Score
- Income
- Credit Utilization/History

What a Balance Is

- The total amount you owe on your credit card.
- If you don't pay the full balance by the due date, interest gets added.
- APR is usually 15%–25%, much higher than most loans.

How Debt Builds

- Paying only the minimum can take years to pay off small purchases.
- Example: $1,000 at 20% APR → only paying $25/mo = ~6 years and $700+ in interest.
- Debt snowballs fast if you keep spending.

Smart Credit Habits

- Pay your full statement balance every month.
- If not possible, pay above the minimum.
- Keep your balance under 30% of your limit.
- Start with just one beginner-friendly card.

QUICK TIP

Treat your credit card like a convenience tool, not a loan. If you can't pay it off in full, rethink the purchase.

Mini Checklist

☐ Be 18+ with income (or 21+ without).

- ☐ Compare beginner-friendly cards.
- ☐ Only apply for one card at a time.
- ☐ Always pay on time.
- ☐ Know your APR.
- ☐ Avoid carrying a balance.
- ☐ Keep balances below 30% of your limit.

Takeaway Quote

"A credit card isn't free money — it's borrowed money. Carrying a balance is like paying rent to the bank for money you already spent."

Visuals

Best First Card Options

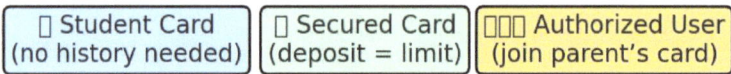

| ☐ Student Card (no history needed) | ☐ Secured Card (deposit = limit) | ☐☐☐ Authorized User (join parent's card) |

What Lenders Look At

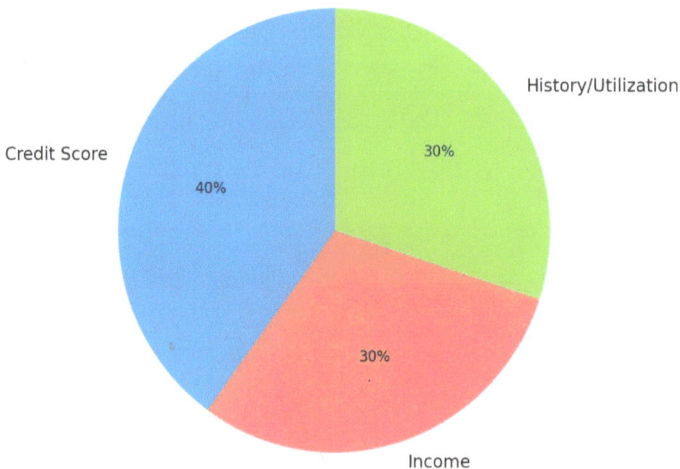

History/Utilization 30%

Credit Score 40%

Income 30%

Paying Off $1,000 at 20% APR

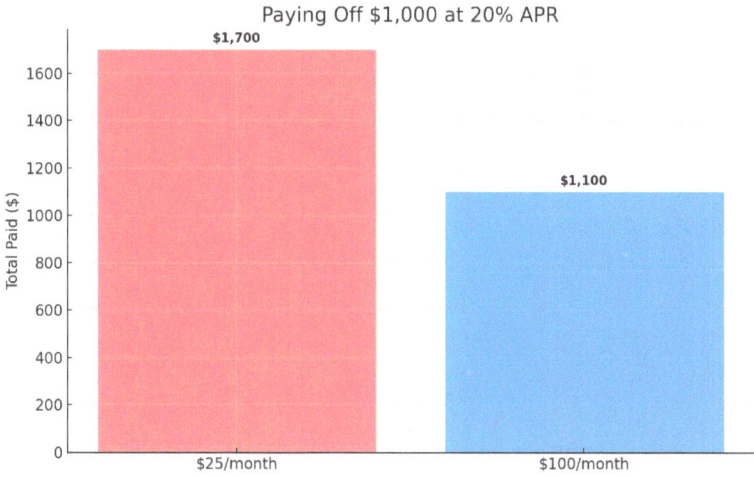

Balance vs. Credit Limit Gauge

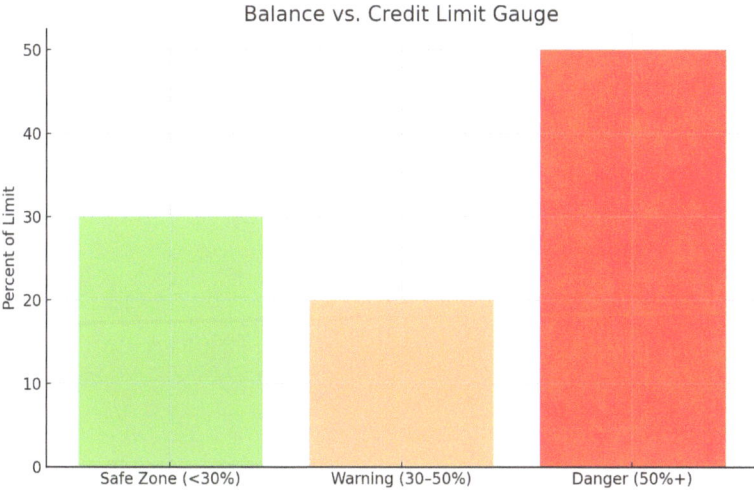

Credit Card Reminder

🡒 Quick Tip:
Don't treat your credit card like free money!

04

WHAT IS INTEREST?

Interest is the price of money. Borrow it, and you pay. Save or invest it, and you earn. Understanding interest is like learning the rules of the game — because it never sleeps.

Two Types of Interest

- **Simple Interest:** Based only on the original amount (the principal).
- **Compound Interest:** Based on the principal plus all the interest earned so far — interest on top of interest.

Why It Matters

- Debt grows faster than you think when interest piles up.
- Investments grow bigger the earlier you start saving.
- The difference between paying 20% on a credit card vs. earning 7% in an index fund is life-changing.

Real-Life Examples

- **Credit Card:** Borrow $1,000 at 20% ➜ if unpaid, can balloon to $1,200+ in a year.

- **Savings Account:** Deposit $1,000 at 2% ➜ grows to only $1,020 in a year.
- **Index Fund:** Invest $1,000 at 7% ➜ grows to about $2,000 after 10 years, $4,000 after 20 years.

Mini Checklist

☐ Learn the difference between APR (loans) and APY (savings).

☐ Pay off high-interest debt first.

☐ Start saving early — let interest work for you, not against you.

Takeaway Quote

"Interest doesn't sleep. Make sure it's working on your side."

Visuals

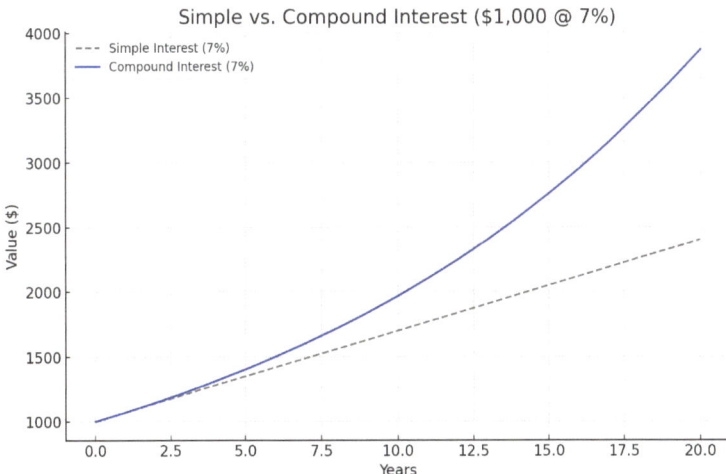

Simple vs. Compound Interest ($1,000 @ 7%)

Debt vs. Investment: $1,000 Example

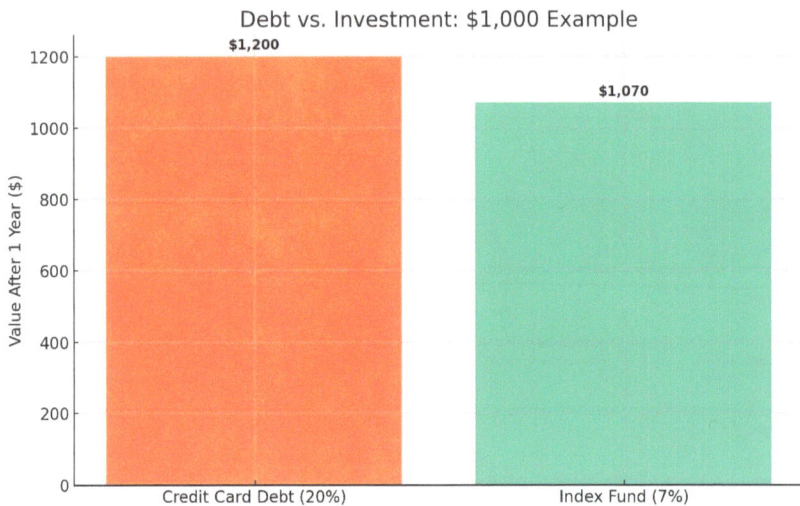

Bar chart titled "Debt vs. Investment: $1,000 Example"; y-axis "Value After 1 Year ($)" from 0 to 1200. Orange bar "Credit Card Debt (20%)" = $1,200; green bar "Index Fund (7%)" = $1,070.

APR vs. APY Cheat Sheet

APR = Cost of borrowing (loans/credit cards)

APY = Earnings from savings (includes compounding)

Quick Tip Reminder

 Quick Tip:
Ask the interest rate
before you borrow or invest!

05

CARS, LOANS, AND INSURANCE

Cars are exciting — but the money side of driving is just as important as the car itself. Whether you're buying, leasing, or insuring, the choices you make can save you thousands (or cost you thousands).

Buying vs. Leasing vs. Used/Pre-Owned

Buying New:

- Latest tech, warranty, zero miles.
- Huge depreciation (~20% loss in the first year).
- Down Payment: 10–20% recommended.

Buying Used/Pre-Owned:

- Lower upfront cost, slower depreciation.
- Certified Pre-Owned (CPO) adds warranty + inspection.
- Older cars may need more maintenance.

- Down Payment: 10–20% recommended.

Leasing:

- Lower monthly payments, new car every 2–3 years.
- No ownership — you give it back.
- Extra costs for damage, excess wear, or mileage overage ($0.15–$0.25 per mile).
- Down Payment: Usually first month + fees + security deposit.

Auto Loans 101

- Loan covers car price minus down payment.
- Terms usually 36–72 months.
- **Key Terms:** Principal, APR, Loan-to-Value (LTV), Depreciation.

Smart Borrowing Tips:

- Put down at least 10–20%.
- Keep term short (3–4 years).
- Don't roll extras into loan.
- Always know your APR.

QUICK TIP:

Longer loan = smaller monthly payment but much higher total cost.

Financing Options: Dealership vs. Bank vs. Credit Union

- **Dealership Financing:** Easiest, but may push higher rates & add-ons.
- **Bank Loan:** Reliable if you've got good credit.

- **Credit Union:** Usually best rates and flexible terms for members.

Car Insurance Basics

- **Liability:** Covers others' damage/injury.
- **Collision:** Repairs your car after accident.
- **Comprehensive:** Theft, fire, weather, animals.
- **Uninsured/Underinsured Motorist:** Covers you if other driver has no insurance.
- **Medical/PIP:** Helps with medical bills.

What Affects Premiums: Age, driving history, car type, location, credit score.

Smart Tips:

- Compare 3+ quotes.
- Raise deductible if you've got emergency savings.
- Bundle for discounts.
- Keep a clean record.

Affordability Rule of Thumb

- Car loan + insurance + gas + maintenance ≤ 15% of your monthly income.
- Don't let car costs push your total debt above 40% of income.

Mini Checklist

- ☐ Compare buying new vs. used vs. leasing.
- ☐ Save for down payment.
- ☐ Shop around: banks & credit unions, not just dealer.
- ☐ Budget for insurance + gas + maintenance.
- ☐ If leasing, plan for mileage + wear/tear fees.

Takeaway Quote

> *"A car gets you places — but the loan, lease, and insurance can trap you. Be smart, and your car will drive your life forward, not backward."*

Visuals

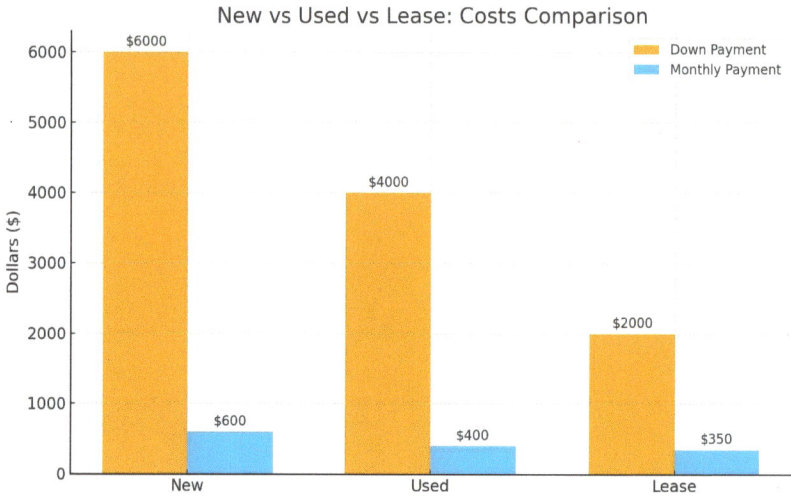

New vs Used vs Lease: Costs Comparison

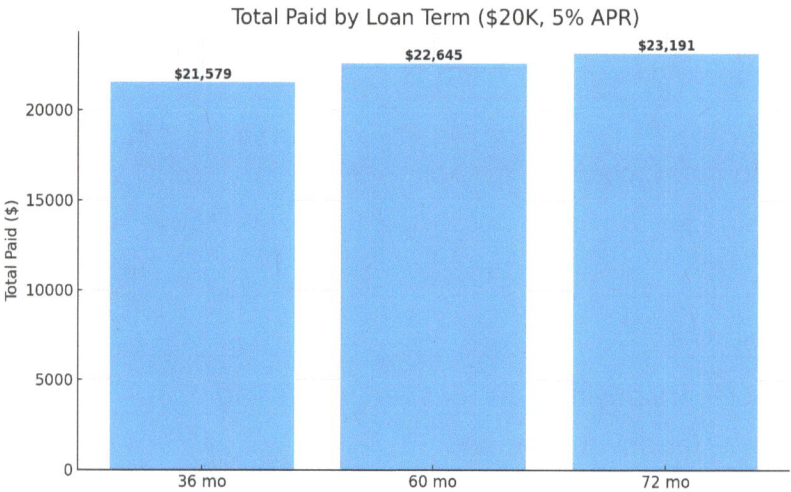

Total Paid by Loan Term ($20K, 5% APR)

Financing Options Compared

🏢 Dealership	🏦 Bank Loan	🏛 Credit Union
Convenient, but highe	Good if you have c	Often best rates & terms

Typical Car Insurance Policy Breakdown

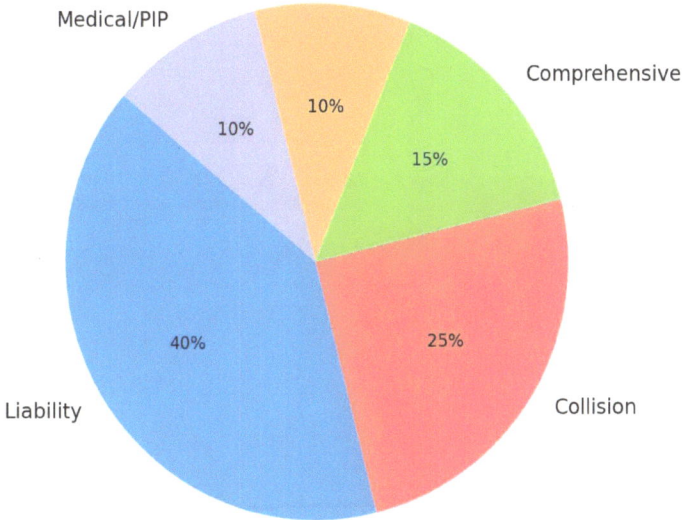

Uninsured

Medical/PIP

Comprehensive

10%

10%

15%

40%

25%

Liability

Collision

Car Costs Reminder

💡 Quick Tip:
Keep car costs ≤15% of income.
Watch lease mileage & damage fees!

06

STUDENT LOANS

Student loans can open the door to college — but they can also feel like a backpack full of bricks if you don't plan ahead. Borrowing for your education isn't "bad," but borrowing blindly is.

Types of Student Loans

Federal Loans (Best First Choice):

- Fixed interest rates
- Flexible repayment plans
- Subsidized ➜ government pays interest while in school
- Unsubsidized ➜ interest starts right away
- Guaranteed ➜ repayment required (they don't just "go away")

Private Loans:

- Higher, variable rates
- Fewer protections
- Harder repayment if you hit trouble

Key Terms to Know

- **Principal:** Amount borrowed
- **Interest Rate (APR):** Cost of borrowing
- **Grace Period:** Usually 6 months after graduation before payments start
- **Default:** Missing payments long-term = damaged credit + collections

Why Student Loans Matter

- They're often necessary to afford higher education.
- They are **federally guaranteed** — meaning you can't just walk away.
- Making payments on time helps you **build credit history** for future loans or rentals.

Smart Borrowing Tips

- Borrow only what you need, not the maximum offered
- Start with federal loans before private
- Make small payments while in school if possible
- Compare repayment options: Standard, Income-Driven, Extended

Quick Example

Borrow $20,000 at 5% ➡ Total repaid = $25,000+.

Make extra payments early? You'll save thousands in interest.

Mini Checklist

- ☐ Apply for FAFSA early
- ☐ Understand subsidized vs. unsubsidized
- ☐ Calculate monthly payments before signing

- ☐ Avoid private loans unless necessary
- ☐ Pay on time to build credit history

Takeaway Quote

"Student loans are an investment in yourself — but only if you borrow wisely."

Disclaimer

This chapter is for **educational purposes only**. Everyone's situation is different. Always **seek professional financial advice** before making borrowing decisions.

Visuals

Student Loan Timeline

Borrowing → Grace Period → Repayment → Paid Off

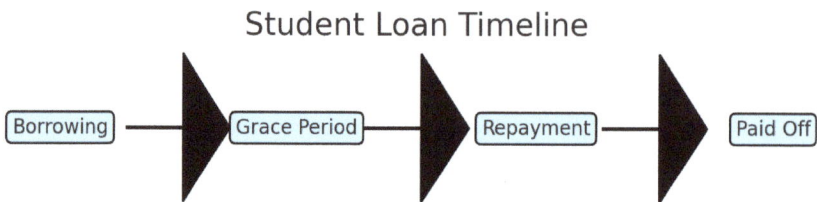

Student Loan Distribution (U.S.)

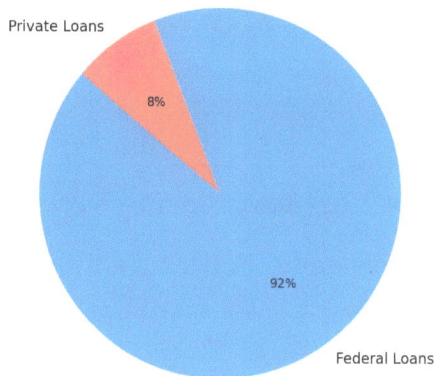

Private Loans

8%

92%

Federal Loans

Cost of $20K Loan at 5% Over 10 Years

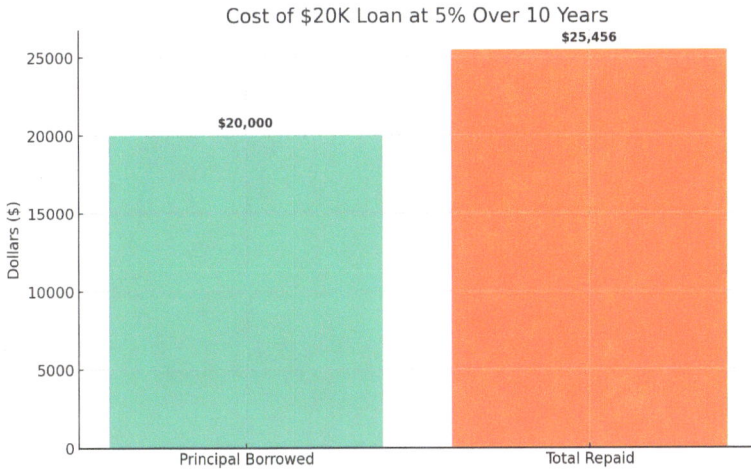

Bar chart comparing Principal Borrowed ($20,000) and Total Repaid ($25,456), with Dollars ($) on the y-axis.

Repayment Plan Comparison (Sample $20K Loan)

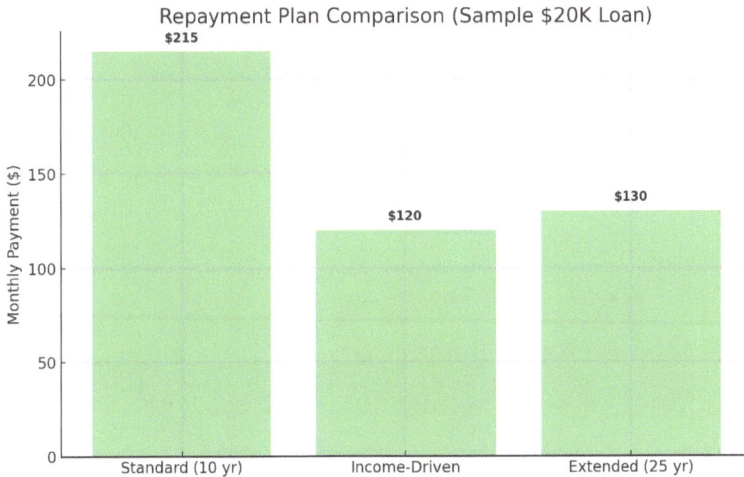

Bar chart comparing Monthly Payment ($) across Standard (10 yr) $215, Income-Driven $120, and Extended (25 yr) $130.

Loan Reminder

⏰ Quick Tip:
Every $1 borrowed = $1 + interest.
On-time payments build credit!

07

RENTING AN APARTMENT

Getting your first apartment feels like freedom — but it comes with fine print. Rent isn't just "monthly payment," it's deposits, fees, insurance, utilities, and sometimes roommates.

What You'll Need Upfront

- **First Month's Rent:** Standard.
- **Last Month's Rent:** Sometimes required.
- **Security Deposit:** Usually 1 month's rent.
- **Application Fee:** $25–$75.

What Landlords Look At

- Credit Score
- Income (usually 3x monthly rent)
- Rental History
- Background Check

Renters Insurance

- Covers **your belongings** (landlord's insurance only covers the building).
- Covers **liability** if someone gets hurt in your place.
- Often required by landlords, usually $15–$30/month.

Utilities & Hidden Costs

- Not all leases include utilities. You may need to pay for:
- Electricity, Gas, Water, Trash
- Internet, Cable, Streaming
- Always ask what's included in rent vs. separate.

Roommates: The Good & The Bad

Pros: Splits rent & utilities, makes housing affordable, built-in social life.

Cons: Less privacy, risk if they don't pay, lifestyle conflicts.

- Always put both names on the lease so everyone is legally responsible.

QUICK TIP

If rent + utilities + insurance = more than 30% of your income, consider a roommate or a smaller place.

Mini Checklist

- ☐ Save for first + last month + deposit.
- ☐ Check your credit before applying.
- ☐ Ask which utilities are included.
- ☐ Get renters insurance.
- ☐ Consider roommates (but choose wisely).

Takeaway Quote

Disclaimer

This chapter is for **educational purposes only**. Rental rules, insurance laws, and housing costs vary by state and landlord. Always **read your lease carefully** and seek **professional advice** for your situation.

Visuals

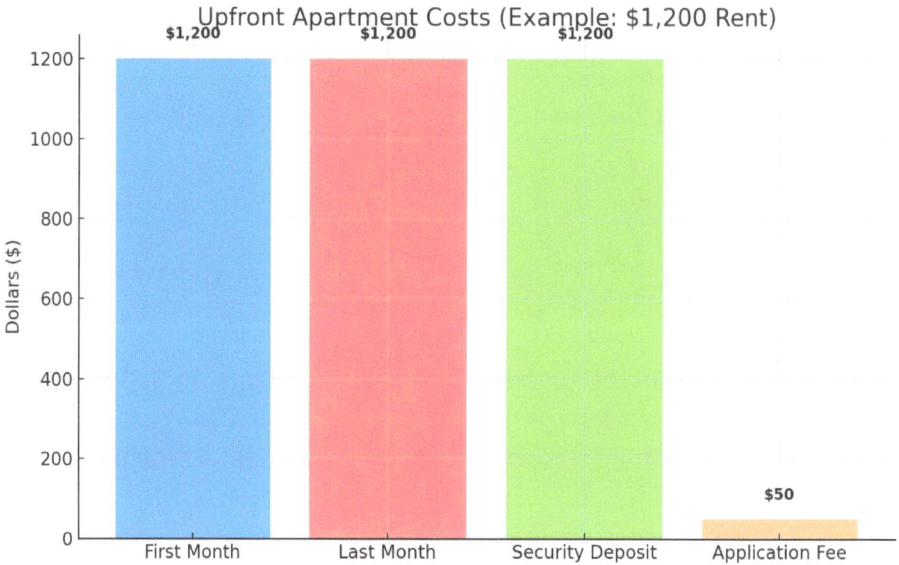

Upfront Apartment Costs (Example: $1,200 Rent)

Monthly Housing Budget Breakdown

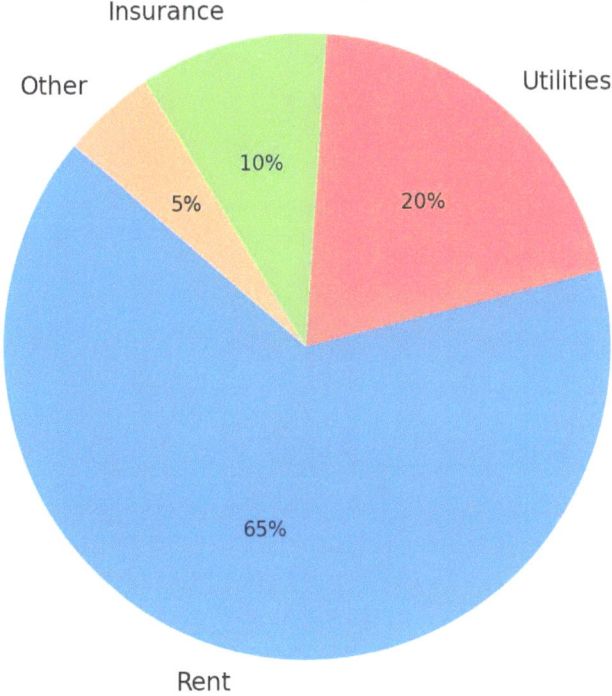

Insurance

Other

Utilities

10%

5%

20%

65%

Rent

Roommate Rent Split (Example $1,200)

You
$600 Rent

Roommate
$600 Rent

Renting Reminder

Quick Tip:
Keep rent + utilities + insurance ≤30% of incom

08

BUYING A HOUSE

Buying a home is one of the biggest financial decisions you'll ever make. It's exciting, but it's also complex. The key is understanding the upfront costs, the loan behind it, and the long-term commitment.

What You'll Need Upfront

- **Down Payment:** 5–20% of price
- 5% = $25,000
- 10% = $50,000
- 20% = $100,000
- **Closing Costs:** 2–5% ($10K–$25K)
- **Earnest Money:** 1–3% ($5K–$15K)

Mortgage Basics

Your monthly payment (PITI) includes:

- **Principal** – loan balance
- **Interest** – cost of borrowing

- **Taxes** – ~$5–$7.5K/year on a $500K home
- **Insurance** – homeowner's (~$1.5–$2.5K/year)
- **PMI** if down <20%

Loan Options & Example Payments ($400K loan)

- **30-Year Fixed @ 7%:**
- ~$2,660/mo
- ~$958K total (nearly 2x loan)
- **15-Year Fixed @ 6%:**
- ~$3,375/mo
- ~$607K total (saves ~$350K)
- **- 5/1 ARM @ 5% (reset to 7%):**
- ~$2,147/mo initially
- Risk of rising payments
- Extra payments can shorten the loan and save interest.

Affordability & Debt-to-Income Rules

- Housing ≤30% of income
- All debt ≤40% of income (mortgage + car + student loans)

Smart Tips

- Get pre-approved before shopping
- Don't buy more house than you can afford
- Save for repairs/maintenance (~1–2% yearly = $5–$10K)
- Fixed-rate loans safer for first-time buyers

QUICK TIP

A 30-year loan looks affordable monthly, but you'll pay nearly double.

Mini Checklist

☐ Save for down + closing costs

☐ Compare loan types

☐ Stick to ≤30% income on housing

☐ Budget for insurance + repairs

Takeaway Quote

"A house isn't just a home — it's a long-term contract with your future self. Buy wisely."

Disclaimer

This chapter is for **educational purposes only**. Everyone's housing market and financial situation is different. Always consult a **licensed mortgage professional or financial advisor** before making decisions.

Visuals

Down Payment Amounts on $500K Home

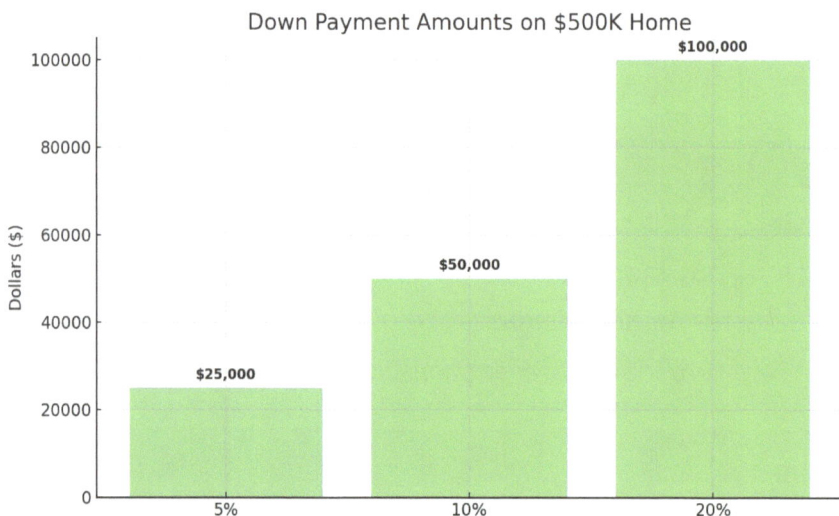

Monthly Mortgage Payment Breakdown (PITI)

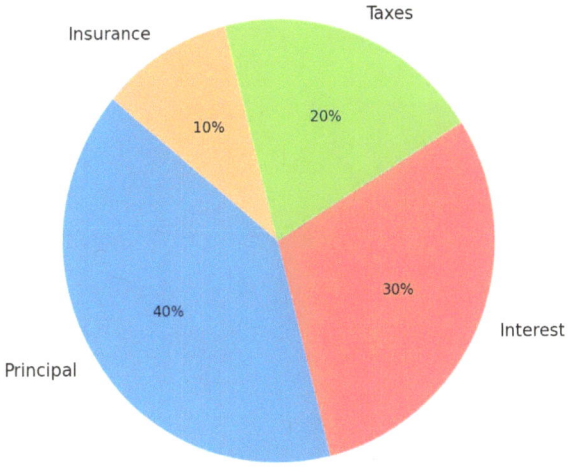

- Insurance 10%
- Taxes 20%
- Interest 30%
- Principal 40%

Loan Type Monthly Payment Comparison ($400K Loan)

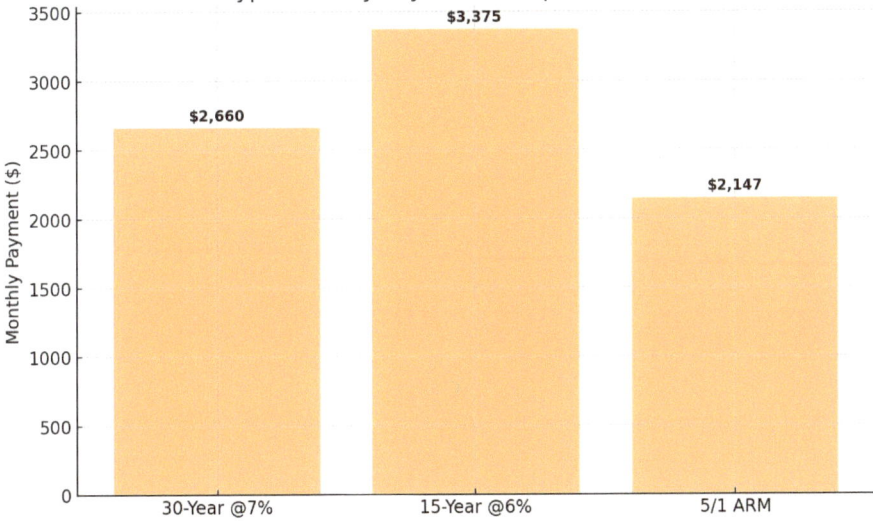

Loan Type	Monthly Payment
30-Year @7%	$2,660
15-Year @6%	$3,375
5/1 ARM	$2,147

Total Loan Cost Comparison ($400K Loan)

1e6

$958,000

$607,000

Total Paid Over Life of Loan ($)

30-Year @7%   15-Year @6%

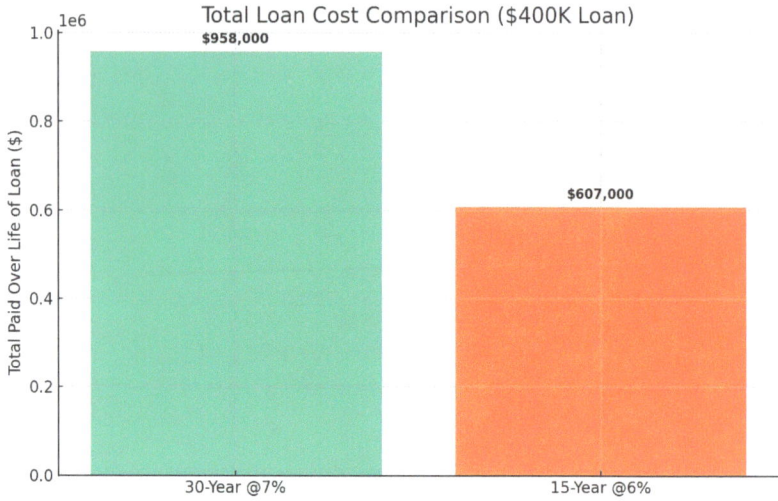

Debt-to-Income Example Breakdown

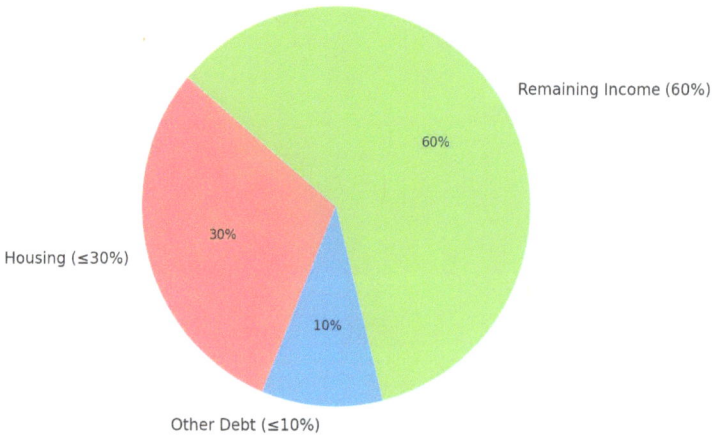

Remaining Income (60%)

60%

Housing (≤30%)

30%

10%

Other Debt (≤10%)

Home Buying Reminder

⬜ Quick Tip:
Housing ≤30%, all debt ≤40%.
Extra payments = big savings!

09

SAVING & BUILDING WEALTH

Saving and investing is how you turn your paycheck into future freedom. The earlier you start, the more time your money has to grow. But before we get into the tools, one big note: there's no "one-size-fits-all." Everyone's situation, goals, and risk tolerance are different.

Important Disclaimer

This chapter is for **educational purposes only**. We are **not giving financial, legal, or tax advice**. You should always meet with a **licensed financial advisor, CPA, or attorney** before making any investment decisions.

The Buckets of Money

Short-Term (safe, liquid): Checking, savings, CDs, money market. Medium-Term: Bonds, muni bonds, balanced mutual funds.

Long-Term (growth): Stocks, index funds, retirement accounts.

Basic Accounts & Safety Nets

Checking, Savings, Money Market, CDs. Brokerage accounts for investing.

FDIC vs SIPC: FDIC covers bank deposits, SIPC covers brokerage accounts if firm fails (not investment losses).

Emergency Fund: 3–6 months expenses before investing.

Stocks & Markets

Stocks = ownership in a company. Penny stocks = high risk.

Stock markets: NYSE (1792), NASDAQ, global exchanges. Sectors: Tech, Healthcare, Energy, etc.

Historical return: ~10% annually.

Bonds & Fixed Income

Corporate, Treasuries, Municipal Bonds, Double Tax-Free Munis. Safer than stocks, returns ~3–5%.

Mutual Funds & Index Funds

Mutual Funds: Managed pools, higher fees. Index Funds: Track a market index, low fees. Sector Funds: Tech, energy, etc.

Fees: 0.03%–1.5% (higher fees eat into returns).

Retirement Accounts

401(k), 403(b), 457, Pensions. IRAs: Traditional vs Roth.

Average returns: 7–8% annually over long term.

Insurance-Based Investments

Whole Life Insurance: slow growth, guaranteed payout. Variable Life: mixes investing + insurance, high fees.

Borrowing Against Life Insurance: You can take loans from cash value, but they reduce death benefit and carry costs.

College Savings Plans

529 Plans: Tax-free growth for education, transferable. Coverdell ESAs: Similar, lower contribution limits.

Risk & Tolerance

Low Risk: Savings, CDs, Treasuries. Medium Risk: Bonds, balanced funds.

High Risk: Stocks, penny stocks, sector funds. Diversify to spread risk.

Inflation & Taxes

Inflation averages 2–3% annually, erodes buying power. Investments must outpace inflation.

Taxes: Capital gains, dividends, IRA/401k rules.

Behavioral Side of Money

Fear & greed derail investors. Stick to a plan, don't chase fads. Investing is long-term, not instant.

Alternative Investments

Real Estate: rental income, appreciation, illiquid. REITs: easier entry.

Gold & Silver: hedge against inflation, volatile. Art & Collectibles: value from rarity, illiquid.

Crypto: very high risk, volatile, not for everyone.

Mini Checklist

- ☐ Build an emergency fund first.
- ☐ Separate short-, medium-, and long-term buckets.

- ☐ Always diversify.
- ☐ Understand fees, taxes, and risk.
- ☐ Meet with a professional.

Takeaway Quote

"Wealth isn't built overnight. It's built over time — with patience, consistency, and a plan that fits your life."

Visuals

Asset Class	Avg Annual Return	Notes
Stocks (S&P 500)	~10% (7% after inflation)	High risk, long-term growth
Bonds	~4–5%	Lower risk, steady income
Cash/Savings	~1–2%	Safe, loses to inflation
Gold	~1–2%	Inflation hedge, volatile
Real Estate	~8–9%	Illiquid, market-dependent

Investment Type	Typical Fees	Notes
Index Funds/ETFs	0.03% – 0.20%	Lowest cost, efficient
Mutual Funds (Active)	0.50% – 1.50%	Higher cost, may underperform index funds
Variable Life Insurance	2% – 4%+	Expensive, hidden policy fees
Whole Life Insurance	1% – 2%+	Slow growth, high fees
Brokerage Trades	$0 (most)	Used to be $5–$20

⚠ This is education only.
Meet with a Financial Advisor,
CPA, or Lawyer before investing.

ANGELS

THANK YOU FOR READING

You made it to the end — and that already puts you ahead of most people when it comes to money. Seriously, most adults avoid this stuff until it bites them in the wallet. You? You're learning it early. Gold star ⭐. This guide was never about telling you exactly what to do with every dollar. It's about giving you the tools to make smarter choices so you can avoid the "oops" moments that cost thousands later.

Think of it as financial GPS: you still have to drive, but at least now you know where the potholes are.

Remember:

- Saving a little is better than saving nothing.
- Debt grows faster than you think (don't feed it).
- Compounding is your BFF if you start early.
- And yes, you can still enjoy your matcha latte... just maybe not *every* day.

At Ella's Angels, we believe knowledge is power, and financial literacy is freedom. But more than that, we believe in you. You are capable of building a future where money works for you, not against you. So go out there. Save a little. Invest a little. Ask questions. Make mistakes (small ones). Learn. Grow. And when you're ready — pay it forward and help someone else. That's how we build not just wealth, but community. With love and belief in your future,

- The Ella's Angels Team

www.ingramcontent.com/pod-product-compliance
Lightning Source LLC
Chambersburg PA
CBHW041720200326
41520CB00005B/222